Fall Risk

Cameron Morse

poems

Glass Lyre Press

Copyright © 2018 Cameron Morse
Paperback ISBN: 978-1-941783-42-9

All rights reserved: except for the purpose of quoting brief passages for review, no part of this book may be reproduced or transmitted in any form or by any means, electronic or mechanical, including photocopying, recording, or by any information storage and retrieval system, without permission in writing from the publisher.

Cover art: ©Cameron Morse, courtesy of St. Luke's Imaging Center
Author photo: Faith Hodges
Design & layout: Steven Asmussen
Copyediting: Linda E. Kim

Glass Lyre Press, LLC
P.O. Box 2693
Glenview, IL 60025
www.GlassLyrePress.com

for my wife, Lili

Contents

The Phlebotomist	1
The Mask	2
The Cave	3
Peeling Wallpaper	4
Jack-o'-Lanterns	5
Winter Morning	6
Pregnancy Test	7
Week 6	8
Working in Mother's Garden	9
Lightning in the Brain	10
Anticonvulsant	11
Afterlife of Rain	12
Lacan at the SSA	13
Meditations	14
Beyond the Shadow	15
Little Star: Week 8	16
Late March	17
The Best and Happiest Moments	18
Ultrasound: Week 10	19
On "Saint Francis Adoring a Crucifix" by Guido Reni	20
Sonogram: Week 12	21
One-Sided Conversation	22
Adverse Action Notice	23
Diana	24

Galileo: Week 20	25
Brain Scan	26
The Day of My First Seizure	27
Leaving Colorado	28
Dusting	29
Gliomatosis Cerebri	30
Astrocytoma	31
The Swing Set	32
Love Song for My Radiologist	33
Bakhtin on the Ketogenic Diet	34
Hemiparesis at the Mississippi River Aquarium	35
Rapid Eye Movement: Week 21	36
Remembrance Lake	37
Poe Poem	38
Guideposts	39
Advance Healthcare Directive	40
Afterlife	41
Acknowledgements	43

The Phlebotomist

Don't look, she says,
as the butterfly needle slips

into the crook of my arm,
but I can't help watching

her silver proboscis
pierce the bruise

of weekly blood draws,
the blue blossom

of scar tissue, or how she
hovers above me

like a seamstress searching
for a seam, threading

herself into my bloodstream.
Don't look, she says.

What she means is, if you flinch,
I might miss. I might slip.

I might kiss you, by accident.

The Mask

On my first visit to the Department
of Radiology, Lady Sky slips a sheet

of plastic into her stainless steel basin,
and I close my eyes while she drapes

its wet weave over my face, its limp
latticework adhering to my cheeks.

I lie upon her table like a corpse
getting dressed in a funeral parlor.

She smooths out the wrinkles in my skin.
Her cool fingers trace the contours

of my eyelids, molding a face out of warm
water. "All right, all finished," she says,

peeling off the hardened semblance of myself,
cerecloth full of breathing holes, porous

membrane still dripping. Later, the mask bolts
my head to the cot. It clutches my skull.

The machine arm swivels loud invisible
beams into my brain.

The Cave

Vampire you call me, leaving for work,
me at home on SSI, unemployed.

Vampire for shutting the door
to my study, for lowering

the blinds, for sucking, sucking
you dry: my cook, my bank, my wife.

You're right. I'm not the man you married
anymore: October, taking my Temodar,

quarantined to the basement, on the chemo
couch drained, watching daytime

TV: Jerry Springer, my only light source.
Other than you, of course. You held me

upright so that I could see the screen,
you helped me up the steps, baby

steps, into your icicled birdbath,
your skyful of falling leaves.

Peeling Wallpaper
for my wife

Black mold bruises the drywall
below the wallpaper's white roses
and chrysanthemums.
Just a tag is all it would take
to tear a strip from popcorn
to baseboard, just a spritz to rub off
the undercoat in wet lashes
of yellow skin, baring sheetrock,
a tug to separate us along the seam
between our bodies
where the mycelia has sealed you
to me from our first night to the night
of my first seizure when your scream
tore through the dark rooms like someone
having a nightmare. At Pikes Peak
Regional, waiting on my cat scan,
you crawled into bed beside me
and adhered. It's been three years
since the scan came back,
and you are still waiting
for me to wake you.

Jack-o'-Lanterns

Telling our unborn son, Your father is in heaven,
you wake in the dark,
childless
beside me. My own father falls
silent across the Pacific, emailing less
and less
until I don't hear from him again.

Will his girlfriend send notice? Or will I beat the old man
to death, dying first? I lie awake listening
to my cancer cells
tip-toe
about the living room, a creak in the floorboards
of my brain. In the morning,
I chuck the jack-o'-lanterns into the garbage can.

Their blackening grimaces burst open
in a flurry of flies. At some point
during the night, their faces disappeared. How haunting it is
to think of them there, spilling
candlelight out of carved eyes, while the wick sank down
into its puddle and the fire shuddered, going out, once
and forever.

Winter Morning

What last night's
fight was about

after morning's
scalpel of light

resects the lawn's
last lump

of bedraggled ice,
doesn't matter

anymore. Everything
becomes dormant.

Flowerbeds drown
in unraked oak leaves,

breezes brokering
deals with silence. At last

only sparrows beat
in the evergreen

heart of the yew.

Pregnancy Test

Ever since urine contrailed two evaporation lines,
and the lighter of them materialized
a second horizon undergirding the dark,
and the strip delineated, out of blank

white space, the purple band of your successful
intervention, how can I go back to work
or think any other thought than that
of you? I see you in the geometry

of my life: your line, a tick, a mark, Christ!
child: I see your coming. On chemo, I dreamt
I dug you, blue baby, blue,
out of a snowbank. When my uncontaminated sperm

sat on ice at the cryobank, and your Mother and I
wondered if we could conceive, I dreamt
of scooping snow out of your ear,
scattering foxes into the dark.

Week 6

And the earth was without form, and void; and darkness was upon the face of the deep. And the Spirit of God moved upon the face of the waters.

—Genesis 1:2

Half-inch long little one, good night.
I am waiting to give you a name. I have spent

nearly 30 years waiting, thinking about a name.
In the translucent bulb of your brain, delicate

veins scrag like lightning. The discharge of your first
thoughts thunders upon the horizon, a reverberation

of my own. Son, Daughter, remember that I, too,
have dangled over the face of the waters

without lids or irises, the black gunk of my eyes
mud-blind. One day you will see

what I mean. It's not easy to weave a wreath
around the sun.

Working in Mother's Garden

Down on her knees in the dirt,
no one beside her, no one caring

about the grass that overgrows
the garden stones, the weeds

that penetrate beyond their border,
all those years she prayed for me

and my baby sisters, prayed
against bad men and brain tumors,

the heroin addict stalking her
daughter. Kneading prayers

into the earth, Mom zeroed in
on dandelions and plantains,

crabgrass and chickweed. Today
I am down on my knees, my hands

in her garden gloves, pulling ligaments.
I scrape out the debris of seasons,

the acorns and oak leaves, grow friendly
with grub, pill bugs, earthworms,

angels of the soil. Behind me, grackles
sport for supper the grass.

Lightning in the Brain

A clock and a crucifix dangle from nails
in my cell at Saint Luke's hospital.
The clock twitches, its tic a telltale sign: Things will not
be all right. I'll be stuck like the second hand,
jittering between one second and the next.

Is it the battery? Is it the brain?
I clutch the left side of my face. The current
pulsates. Muscles flinch and flash. Lips
lurch toward the jawline, slurring speech.
Better to be speechless: Why are you sobbing

                    in your mother's arms, saying I'm sorry, I'm sorry?
                        Don't you deserve this? To be split open
                            from the inside like a tree? To be struck black
                  by lightning? There is justice in your jagged scar.
                  She did nothing to deserve you, the lightning jolt,

                    the jerk of her 28-year-old son, except to long
                        for your return, and pray for the strength
                          to climb the shaggy trunk into the branches
            of lightning, and pluck the tumor from your brain.

Anticonvulsant

Little tablet, sky-blue sacrament,
paint chip off the ceiling of a cathedral,

I call you Keppra, my Protector,
Levetiracetam. Twice daily
your splinter of stained glass
passes through the palm of my hand.

Twice daily I accept your gospel
of 250 milligrams,

transubstantiate your body into my blood, your word
into my flesh. I accept
your side effects:

somnolence, decreased
energy, suicide,
salvation.

Afterlife of Rain

Brushstrokes of the oak tree
branch inscribe
in soft air—

    How will I know myself before I'm gone?

Clouds shift imperceptibly
in the white murk
of the cataract.

I cling to life like these raindrops
to the serrated leaf
of the rosebush, my hand

    closed around the blade.

Let me be willing, first,
to recollect nothing
of this earth.

Lacan at the SSA

Waiting to be seen, I cannot say
I know my name: this, Lacan calls *the mirror
stage*. Imaginary, I have not yet

entered through the door, not yet drawn a number
from the machine. The security guard has not
questioned me: What brings you in today?

What, indeed, has brought me here? I lie awake
worrying about line breaks and workshops. At the plexiglass,
I fumble bank statements, my spouse's paystubs,

whisper under the sill, still no employment,
no assets, no weapons of any kind. Unable to recall my Mother's
maiden name, I exit, disvalued,

undesired, driven by—my Mother,
Anger—the binder bulging with uncalled-for documents,
medical reports, poems.

Meditations

You will soon be dead, and you are not yet simple, or unperturbed.

—Marcus Aurelius

A dark patch of lawn studded with fallen apples, gashed
apples browning to the mush.

Not yet dead, I stand, letting the rain tick
off my forehead. This,

an impromptu therapy session, a baby rhino
chopped to pieces

beside the body of its mother. Hayden Carruth, age 53,
giving his first reading. My stomach

turning after last night's Temodar.
Rain falling on rotten apples.

Beyond the Shadow

Chemo bald as a light bulb,
the dent in my head a dark ravine,
a valley of the shadow. I trace
the incision with my fingertips

unable to recollect the drill twirling
a hole into my skull, the stereotactic
needle piercing my right hemisphere.
The anesthetic took me. Counting

down from ten, I slurred seven.
Before the results came back
from Nebraska, twice-checked,
just in time for the appointment,

my tumor might have been benign,
as they say, or slow-growing, inching
like lichen. I might have continued
to saunter, soaking up the sunlight,

the squirrels and the gumballs along
Golfview Drive—playing board games
with my brother, making love
with my wife—which is not to say

I have forsaken my place in the light
of this world, but I have learned
what it means to abide.

Little Star: Week 8

Embryo son, fetus daughter, wherever
you are in your path of orbit, hear
me: I am dying. My brain tumor

is bigger than you are. It is all
the stars together, packed into a snowball
searing bare hands. I could never

say this to your mother, that saintly
apparitional being I so unworthily
married, who hasn't for a moment

doubted living to be old together,
but if I'm not standing there in my sky
blue gown as you fall headfirst

into the light of this world, then
I passed you on my way out,
grazing your cheek with my blazing tail.

Late March

Crab apple trees blossom,
sprinkling pink white
petals over the dark,

tire-treaded silt of the curb
and the lawn's mangy
grass. Blackbirds cackle

around the cul-de-sac,
their dark silhouettes
entangled in the tracery

of branches, and petals
pattern the driveway
like braille, a language of

fingers, figures discerning
in the dark of what it feels like
today's sky draped with

linens, cold rain prickling
the back of my neck
like a guillotine.

The Best and Happiest Moments

Poetry is a record of the best and happiest moments of the happiest and best minds.

—Percy Bysshe Shelly

Midnights when my mattress drifts,
and the grandfather clock tolls

out of its oaken hollow, I call you Nightingale.
You, who sat in the dark and sang,

died at 29 and here I am the same age,
reading your *Defence*, defenseless,

in my third October since diagnosis.
I have followed every recommendation—

from chemo to radio beams—but still
feel my *footsteps like those of a wind*

over the sea, the Gulf of La Spezia,
perhaps, or the gulf between us,

between drowning, swallowed in seaweed,
and taking Temodar. Still I, too, have lived

by the sea. I have seen linen clouds billowing
on the clothesline. I have smelt the salt

sea air. I, too, have made recordings.

Ultrasound: Week 10

You shimmer
at the bottom of a well,

little light, caught
on a crest of dark water,

rocking. You rock as she walks,
as your Mother reclines. Yoga pants

pulled below her pubic bone, black
tuft peeking above her waistline, she unfolds

her driving and movie-going glasses
and peers with me at the exam room screen.

The stirrups of a Midmark 623 hold her feet,
her knees, apart. Lady Sky's transducer

sleds through water-soluble gel, its nose
irradiating inaudible sound

waves like a dolphin until—is it just me—or
is that you kicking your leg

buds? Your heartbeat, a thunder
too faint for my ears, flickers

on the far horizon.

On "Saint Francis Adoring a Crucifix" by Guido Reni

Last night, at Inklings'
Books and Coffee Shoppe,

when you asked if I was ever going
to stop writing cancer poems

and pursue other subjects, I thought
of Saint Francis tonsured

at the Nelson-Atkins,
his cadaverous hands folded

over his breast like wings, how the right
hand rests upon the left, as if

to perform CPR on his own stopped
heart, the breath sucked

out of his lungs, his eyes flung
open at the moment of arrest, the moment

arrested, and may you never know
what it's like to be transfixed,

for you to don a stitched
cassock and waft like a dove

caught in the updraft, caught up
in the representation of a death

which is also your own.

Sonogram: Week 12

Today I tuned in to the fetal doppler and heard
your heartbeat for the first time. Seated

among stainless steel escutcheons, coat hooks
and carts loaded with specimen cups and tampons,

I heard your 160 beats per minute crackle
over the speakers, the inaudible sound of you

transduced into jackhammer, marching drum,
hummingbird, the sonogram of a Sunday morning

wind seen as ocean waves flattening the grass, praises
sung from the cloister of crab apple, Japanese maple

and plum, their coffers full of petals,
emptied out on the ground.

One-Sided Conversation

Your call may be
monitored for quality

assurance. Your wait may
exceed the single-digit number

of years that you have left.
But then you've been

waiting—haven't you?—ever
since the diagnosis, for life

to begin again, so it's not as if
you're alive now anyway.

You belong here with me, holding
or being held by a woman

who may or may not be
a machine.

Adverse Action Notice

Send us your bank statements,
your paystubs, your ontological
arguments, or else we will shut
your file down. Walmart pharmacy
will forget your prescription.

After the last two days of tablets,
the last two days of shelter
from lightning-strike seizures,
the embarrassment of convulsing
like a Pentecostal, you may find

yourself drooling in front of your
friends or back at the Family
Support Division at 8 a.m., sitting
in a row of scratched captain's
chairs from which jurors

delivered death sentences 20 years ago:
Please Take a Number lettered
above the bulletproof windowpane
in which your interviewer—blond
mustache, Bass Pro T-shirt—yawns,

puttering. 11a.m: *Call Melissa,* scratched
with a quarter in the bathroom stall:
$25 BJ's. You have only four tablets
left, an MRI scan in two days.

Diana

Diana, this time, fetches me before sunrise
from the waiting room at Saint Luke's Imaging.

Diana, hunter goddess of the moon,
leads me into her inner chamber and straps

a tourniquet to my bicep. I squeeze her
rubber ball. To get my blood up, I pump my fist.

The silver tip of her arrow glances off the wall
of my vein like a moonbeam. This, she calls,

"advancing the catheter." She swabs
the inkblot of my blood with alcohol and fires again.

I know the drill like a centurion, scar tissue
inveterate, on methylprednisolone and Benadryl.

In the machine room Diana pulls off my glasses
and lays them on her stainless-steel nightstand.

The coil chiller chirps. Its apiary birdsong
lulls me to ease my neck into her lunette,

her crescent moon. My bracelet says FALL
RISK as my feet lift off the ground.

Galileo: Week 20

During the second ultrasound
I sit with her in planetary
dark. I sit beside her table

in my chair. On screen a shining
circle encompasses our son's
cerebrum, our son Theo.

We know his name now. We know
he is a he. His penis gleams,
his corona of glans. We gaze

upon his celestial body, his lips
and forehead rising
like Jupiter in the night sky.

Brain Scan

Reminds me of the night
of my first seizure. A moth

fluttering like an eyelid, batting
at the overhead in a Cripple Creek

ambulance, the light of a mineshaft
seconds before cave in. My EMT,

tongue-in-cheek, says, "Looks like
we picked up a passenger." A Lady

of the Night, in the black and white
of the brain on screen, I see her

shifting, the dim tumble of my moth
beating frayed wings.

Today's theme is *recurrence*, what
the radiologist sees, the brindled

skirt of the lady I carry, folded
like a handkerchief in gray matter.

The Day of My First Seizure

In the morning I listened as the country mountain preacher cast down arguments and every high thing, then went with friends into Cripple Creek and ate a burnt hamburger among the rundown casinos. I wanted to spot the ancestral donkeys of the first gold miners which the town's folk allow to range. The shame of it is, I didn't, and at the Heritage Museum wearied of prospector stories. At an ice-cream shop, I treated everybody to a scoop but me. A hailstorm sprang upon the two-lane highway back to Florissant. Ice balls burst into stars upon the windshield. Halfway up the gravel drive, I climbed out into the rain wearing a sister's sunbonnet to meet an antlered mule deer that was curled up below the Ponderosa pines. It returned my gaze. Moss-splotched slabs of pink granite darkened around us. Saucers of sugar water dangled from the ranch house eaves and hummingbirds tangled for dominion. After dark, lightning forked over Pike's Peak. The bones of dead deer flared up below the deck rail where I stood, scanning the twilit rise for mountain lions.

Leaving Colorado

On the day before departure, I will ask
once more to hear the sound of Falling River
flowing through Estes Village
below my balcony rail, its *hush, hush,*

now. It's time to go. Once more observe
the clouds drape their giant shadows
over the alpine ridge, the black-streaked
clouds dragging white tassels over the saw

teeth of the pines. One more day and I might
have ascended through Douglas firs
to the black glacial lakes called Nymph,
Emerald, Dream, and spread out my body

for chipmunks and magpies to eat
one final vision out of my eyes:
That of you, my wife, the wind blowing
your black hair into my mouth.

Dusting

I turn lamb's wool around the storm door
cobwebbed during my absence,

seeing what the world will look like
without me, what spiders

will take hold without my hand
on the knob, tiny weavers whispering

at the loom of moonlight.
During my absence, Virginia creeper

drapes its jacket of serrated
blades over my garden's irises

and zinnias, soaking up the sun
in their stead, smothering my flowers

in their own bed. It lies like a sleeping
parent over the baby's breath.

Gliomatosis Cerebri

Threads, like the white vermiculate
roots of the tomato plant
in my Mother's hands, infiltrate,
filtering in
to my brain substance.

At sunset in her garden, she loosens
the boxed fists of soil, pearls
of fertilizer falling into spade holes.
Threads of glial cells slip down
while the sky darkens around us.

I sit in the lawn chair of my life,
watching her work. The sky comes
into focus: Astrocytes, stars oft compared
to needlepoints, poke
fun at me, the poet, embroidering

their stick figures into the fabric
of my brain: Aries, the constellation
of my birth; Cancer, the unknown,
known—because of its obscured
visibility—as the dark sign.

Astrocytoma

Jeff, a former navy man,
rides a butterfly

needle into my vein.
His line leaps with my red

river of platelets, lymphocytes,
white blood cells.

*How long does it take
to become a phlebotomist?*

He shakes the vial, a cocktail
of yellow gunk and blood,

his arm a blurred mermaid,
mine a bruised creek,

the scar tissue still dark
from last Tuesday.

About eight weeks, he says.
It took me ten years,

I'm told, to grow my astro-
cytoma the size of a golf ball.

On night watch, he says
I used to drive golf balls

*off the edge of the USS
Gerald R. Ford,* satellites

arcing through the stars.

The Swing Set

Deep in the shade of my third year
since diagnosis,
swing set rafters web
above the blackened planks.
Cicada casings cling to its undercarriage,
their bodies missing.
I can no longer hear them
screaming. The cricket hums to itself
its tiny lamentation. Autumn comes,
and my bimonthly visit with the oncologist
is tomorrow morning, a wheelbarrow
to be pushed from the wood pile
to the back patio, unloaded
and pushed back again.

Love Song for My Radiologist

I stand at the cast-iron bars of the storm door
to my study, the bars that open to sunrise, inundated by daylight

into late morning, looking up into the rose of Sharon
branches that mantle my comings and goings.

My radiologist Anastasia on mysaintlukes.org reports:
No evidence of disease progression. A cascade of leafy vines

dangles over my dented forehead. In the shadow of my incision,
a mourning dove weaves her basket of yellow grass and mud,

integrating packing tape and hospital bracelets
into a nest for hatchlings. Then fledglings. Then doves.

Bakhtin on the Ketogenic Diet

Deep breaths, autumn's
empty birdbath.

Zinnias loosen
their balled fists, sprinkling

petals over yellow grass.
Death camps become

tourist destinations, my brain
scans monologic,

regulatory. I almost feel
correct. I could start again.

I have no reason to stay
on the diet

if all I am is a wind
sifting through the treetops,

looking for a lost passage,
a living language.

Hemiparesis at the Mississippi River Aquarium

Clawing, I manage
at least partially

to roll up one sleeve
and slide a hand

into the Touch Tank.
Cownose stingrays flap

brown angelic wings
over to me. Slick

rough hides arch
into the palm

of my palsied hand.
White breasts press

the glass. In the gaze
of those awkward

black eyes, I see
a yearning

that mirrors my own
to be touched,

to be stung.

Rapid Eye Movement: Week 21

The first time I felt him kick,
she took my hand in a movie theater
and placed it on her lower abdomen.
In *National Geographic* I read

his eyes have begun to flicker
below closed lids. About fifteen minutes
into *The Mummy,* when Ahmanet
bumps the lid off her sarcophagus,

he started kickboxing skeletons. I felt him
dreaming among dreamers, families
of us, my wife and I with our eyes open,
scintillating in the footlit dark.

Remembrance Lake

The splashdown of a shorebird
irradiates to the algae-green

sludge of the water's edge, stroking
driftwood, cutting clefts.

The water forgets. But this leafless
locust still carries the galls

that killed it, the fists of crust
where wood wasps oviposited

and the tumor still incubates
in the hatchery of my brain.

Poe Poem

Because of the mask that molded to my face during the fitting, hardening
as the warm water dried, the mask that fastened
my head to the cot, and because of the cot that carried me into the machine,
the BEAM that unloaded a single dose of radiation every morning,
Monday through Friday, and because the techs left me alone in there
to take my dose, closing the steel door
behind them, while the robot arm rotated around my head, firing
invisible shots of radiation, I wrote no poems. I had no thoughts.

The radiologist said I would be dead within two years. Ravens
decorated the ceiling panels. I read "The Masque of the Red Death"
on rides to the Department of Radiology, pulling down
my stocking cap over my ears. I shaved my head, grew out my beard.
For the first time in my life, I insisted on carving
jack-o'-lanterns, clawing out
the cold slime of their brains with my fingernails.

Guideposts

The guideposts of the pear
tree I planted last year

in the summer
of dexamethasone slid

down today on the rain-
softened earth, down

below a barricade of clouds.
Pulling with equal strength

in either direction, they
fell inward, crossing each other.

The steroids ruined
the nights I staggered

from chair back to countertop,
kneecaps coruscating

as if gunshot.

Advance Healthcare Directive

Late morning I seat myself
in the pulsating leafy

shade of the crab apple tree.
North wind washes

over my scalp, inspiring the oak
and maple trees

with a breath that fills their
leaves like lungs

on a respirator. I lie down
at the foot of the driveway.

If I am not able to speak
for myself, let me follow

the grackles to the edge
of the birdbath, the rabbit

hopping across the rock bed
of my periphery. If I become

permanently unconscious,
remember me as I am,

the leaves clapping over the pages
of my notebook.

Afterlife

I wake to the twinkling
frost, starlight encrusted

into the lawn. I walk,
eyes watering

eastward, tramp
into unmown shadows

to pinch the slush
off a blade of grass.

Drops of water belly
from tiny budding branches.

Here, unchurched except
by cancer, I am always

at a loss, always a little less
able than I thought to accept

the failure of speech
to encapsulate

meaning, to let my unborn
son plant his hands

on my shaggy cheeks
in the ministry of birdsong.

Acknowledgements

I am grateful to my mentors L.S. Klatt, Hadara Bar-Nadav, and Robert Stewart, to my workshop at Inklings' Books and Coffee Shoppe, my wife, Lili, and my mother, Aunt Cathi and Cousin Bryce; for help with my manuscript, Jessica Goodfellow and Maryfrances Wagner. I am also grateful to the editors in whose magazines the following poems first appeared (some in earlier forms):

The 3288 Review: "Love Song for my Radiologist."

Big Muddy: "Hemiparesis at the Mississippi River Aquarium."

Bridge Eight: "Guideposts."

Caesura: "Brain Scan."

Communion: "Beyond the Shadow," "Anticonvulsant," "Afterlife."

The Cresset: "On "Saint Frances Adoring a Crucifix" by Guido Reni."

Edify Fiction: "Gliomatosis Cerebri."

Fourth & Sycamore: "The Best and Happiest Moments."

From Sac: "Dusting."

Hawaii Pacific Review: "The Cave."

I-70 Review: "Peeling Wallpaper" "Jack-o'-Lanterns" "Remembrance Lake."

New Letters: "The Phlebotomist" "The Mask."

pamplemousse: "Lightning in the Brain."

Perigee: "Adverse Action Notice."

Pirene's Fountain: "Leaving Colorado."

Rogue Agent: "Diana."

Small Print Magazine: "Winter Morning" "Astrocytoma."

Steam Ticket: "Afterlife of Rain."

Third Wednesday: "Ultrasound: Week 10."

The Tishman Review: "The Swing Set."

Two Words For: "Poe Poem."

TYPO: "Day of My First Seizure."

Vector Press: "Bakhtin on the Ketogenic Diet"

The Visitant: "Pregnancy Test" "Week 6" "Working in Mother's Garden."

Whale Road Review: "Little Star: Week 8."

About the Author

Diagnosed with Glioblastoma in 2014, **Cameron Morse** is currently a third-year MFA candidate at the University of Missouri—Kansas City and lives with his wife Lili and newborn son Theodore in Blue Springs, Missouri. His poems have been or will be published in over 75 different magazines, including *New Letters, Bridge Eight, South Dakota Review, I-70 Review* and *TYPO*.

Glass Lyre Press

exceptional works to replenish the spirit

Glass Lyre Press is an independent literary publisher interested in technically accomplished, stylistically distinct, and original work. Glass Lyre seeks diverse writers that possess a dynamic aesthetic and an ability to emotionally and intellectually engage a wide audience of readers.

Glass Lyre's vision is to connect the world through language and art. We hope to expand the scope of poetry and short fiction for the general reader through exceptionally well-written books, which evoke emotion, provide insight, and resonate with the human spirit.

Poetry Collections
Poetry Chapbooks
Select Short & Flash Fiction
Anthologies

www.GlassLyrePress.com

www.ingramcontent.com/pod-product-compliance
Lightning Source LLC
Chambersburg PA
CBHW021159080526
44588CB00008B/418